Log of the Gee Whiz

and

More Short Stories

MEMOIRS, FAIRY TALES, HUMOR, AND INSPIRATION

Joy Sorrell

Manor Publishing Collective
Seattle, Washington

Contents

Preface

The following book is a compilation of the book, *Log of the Gee Whiz,* which I put together as a self-published coffee-table book in 2008, and various other short stories about my life and experiences that were written years ago but never published. I only produced (could afford) enough copies of *Log of the Gee Whiz* to share with my family and close friends, although it was a lovely small hardcover book that I'm sure many more people would have enjoyed.

Years later, in 2020, while living at The Manor for Seniors in San Diego, I learned of Sunny Baker's new venture to professionally publish the memories and stories of senior writers who would like to share them with the public at large but who just didn't have the finances, skills, and/or energy to publish their works at a reasonable price.

I contacted Sunny and showed her a remaining printed copy of the self-published *Log of the Gee Whiz* along with my yellowed, typewritten short stories on aging erasable paper. I asked her if she could publish these in a single volume as a complete book. Her response was, "Yes. I can do that. But I'll have to scan, edit, and format the stories and it might take a little time. I have three books ahead of yours right now."

I asked how much it would cost. She grinned and stated zealously, "It won't cost you a thing now. However, the "collective" will get a portion of your royalties after the work is published." (Manor Publishing Collective is the new publishing company she started in December 2019.)

I was skeptical, but what did I have to lose? The stories had been languishing unread in my files for years already. And I wasn't getting any younger...

I gave her the hardcover book and the typewritten stories, and we signed a contract to have them published as a complete book. Since I wasn't the only author getting Sunny's attention, it took a few months. You are reading the results now.

I look forward to sharing this book with my readers for years and years to come thanks to Sunny Baker and the Manor Publishing Collective.

*Getting Ready for the Launch of the Refurbished **Gee Whiz***

Log of the Gee Whiz

Introduction to The Log

Publisher's Note:

The following is a slightly edited version of the original introduction to Log of the Gee Whiz from the self-published coffee table book produced in 2008.

Recently as I sat at my sewing table working on a project, Devon wandered into the room to browse my bookshelf. Settling himself into the armchair he began to read chapter VI in my first edition copy of *Log of the Gee Whiz.* Amused by the story, he began to read aloud. Pretty soon we were both laughing at the antics of everyone on board.

Reading back over these stories, I was inspired to create a second edition. In 1995 when we first "sorta published" *The Log*, Gary transcribed my father's original log entries, written in the mid-1950s on a portable Royal typewriter, into digital format and printed them out for others to enjoy. There are also pencil drawings I had created that when put together with the text made a pleasant story, complete with illustrations.

When I called my father 13 years later to propose a collaboration on a second edition, I was very pleased to hear that he not only still had the digital files and copies that we created in 1995, but that he also had color 35mm slides documenting many of the events reported in *The Log*.

The second published edition, which I had self-published at some cost using a third-party production house, contains scans of my pencil drawings like the first edition, with the addition of many of the photos and the poem called "Pome (*sic*) for Pop" which I wrote about my father's magical relationship with his boat, the sea, and the fish.

I want to congratulate my father on the Yellowtail and thank him for the first edition and the sleuthing it took to find and digitize the photos and drawings. And I want to thank G. Joy (as she's known to her grandkids) for her creativity in writing and sharing these stories and drawings.

Love,

Carmen Joy

Pop Reeling One In

It started when Jim and I and our small sons, Gary and Greg, moved to San Diego so Jim could get his degree from the State College there. Boats have always been a fascination for all of us, big ones and little ones alike. Now, for the first time near so many snug little yacht harbors, we spent all our free time watching the boats coming and going and dreaming about the day we could call one ours.

Grandpa and Nonie, who lived ninety miles away in Riverside, spent many weekends with us and, after due exposure, Grandpa came down with a bad case of "boat-itis" too. Shortly thereafter, he launched the family in a home- grown 14-foot outboard with a 10-horsepower Mercury motor. Everybody thought this great fun, for a least one week, until the first in a whole series of disasters, known well to all boating enthusiasts as the "we-need-a" bug, fell with a thud. The "disaster" was that 10-horse Merc couldn't make that 14' plywood run-about plane. Now Nonie and I, not wanting to show our ignorance of nautical jargon and thinking "plan" must be something the Coast Guard thought necessary for boating safety, and having stressed the need for safety, agreed: We needed to "plane", whatever that was... Actually, it turns out "planing" occurs when more power (and speed) is applied, lift increases, and the boat, in effect, rides over its bow wave, reducing wetted area and thus reducing drag. At this point, the boat is said to be "on a plane" or simply "planing."

A short trip to a local boat builder and outboard motor sales and service soon let us know what "we needed" was a bigger motor. Just imagine! That 10-horse Merc made just the right trade-in on a 33-horsepower Scott-Atwater. While Nonie and I were in a somewhat dazed condition, Jim and Grandpa formed a partnership. Ultimately, the boat "planed" and the "Scott" was the pride of the family. We christened our beloved little yellow boat the *Rock 'n Row*, a name suggested by six-year-old Gary.

Four little boys made our pleasure complete. Four small orange life jackets were standard gear. My sister-in-law Ernie and I, two very skeptical young mothers, stood on the sand at Dana Landing and wondered how we would decide which little boy to swim for when the boat went over.

For Ernie, this was a huge decision since she couldn't swim. Pretty soon, however, all safe and sound, Grandpa, his son Gene, and his two sons, Mike (four-years-old) and Tiny Tim (one and a half,) and Jim and our two boys, Gary and Greg, would roar up with sun-shiny faces and dump four little boys onshore. Ignoring the young boys' wails you could hear up and down the beach, the three big boys would gaily wave good-bye and a-fishing the whole crew would go. Out in the open sea just as brave as could be, they left we three gals to scrub off the salt spray without touching the sunburn and feed and bed four tired little boys.

Fixing food for the returning fishermen, fibbing to the children about another boat ride before Sunday night, pelleting everybody in a two-bedroom house, and gossiping about all the family members not present (three males in particular,) we whiled away Saturday from early morning 'til dark. Sunday evening as the sun went down, the *Rock 'n Row*, all scrubbed and quiet, was backed into the yard and Grandpa and Nonie and Gene and Ernie, with two sleepy little boys, waved goodbye until the next weekend and started on their two-hour trip home.

I have neglected to mention the best part of the whole affair: The fish! As is usually the case with beginners, our luck was colossal! What does one do with gunnysacks full of fish? Jim and Gene came home, for the most part, with fish we were all familiar with. But not Grandpa. He was always good for a surprise.

One time Grandpa came home with a very large green and bilious looking creature. We diligently filleted it out only to find the meat was the same bilious green. Well, we planted that fish under the apricot tree and, I might add, no apricots grew that year. We found out later, however, the fish was quite a delicacy known as a Cabazon. The tasty meat turns pure white when it is cooked!

Strange green creatures aside, we had plenty of fish to go around. We very generously gave fish to everyone who didn't lock their door and pretend they weren't home. Gene and Ernie packed it in ice and gave some thirty-four Bonita to friends in Pomona.

By this time the fishing fever had overtaken every one of us, from Tiny Tim right on up. Everybody got fishing poles, reels, line, sinkers, etc., for Christmas, birthdays, and any other excuse we could find. Ernie and I were no exception and Grandpa, generous soul that he is, took each of us deep-sea fishing.

My first deep sea fishing trip was an experience I'll never forget. Grandpa was invited on a charter to the Coronado Islands and since Nonie was recuperating from an illness and couldn't go to sea, she stayed with Gary and Greg, and away we went. We had soup and coffee for breakfast at midnight and left the sportfishing dock on a boat called the Can-Do. We left a 1:30 a.m., stopped for bait, and proceeded to the Coronado Islands. I stirred from my nap at about 5:00 a.m. to find Grandpa already had his line wet.

I wandered out to look around. Wow! What I saw! A school of Yellowtail that to me looked like whales swarming around the boat. Everyone was so excited they were bumping into each other and tangling their lines. With Grandpa's help, I got my line in too and through the clear green water, I watched the beautiful big fish swim close to my bait and then turn and swim away.

After about an hour of watching other fishermen, among them Grandpa, land big Yellowtail and still without a single strike of my own, I was beginning to wonder if you had to have "fish-appeal" or something. Just then one of the deckhands, a real nice guy I might add, got a hook-up with a lure, and shouted, "This one's for the little lady!" He handed me a pole on the other end of which was a dynamo headed the other way. My new friend stood by and gave me instructions on where to put the butt of the pole, where to hold, and how to reel, which were: "In your groin!"; "Anywhere you can!"; and "Faster!" That fish and I battled until we were both pooped. I struggled and finally won the battle. With the help of a gaff, my prize was finally on the deck, the most beautiful twenty-pound Yellowtail that ever swam the blue Pacific! I collapsed with a tremendous sense of accomplishment, a ham sandwich, and a cup of coffee.

Fishing is a wonderful sport and certainly a new-found thrill for me, but as we were plowing along on our way home with the warm sun on us and the salt spray in our faces, I decided these fishermen of ours weren't fooling me anymore. Strictly escapism, but how lovely to spend half the night and two-thirds of the day where I couldn't hear anybody shout, "Mama!" But alas—poor Nonie... Someone had to clean the fish.

Our catch on this trip amounted to nine Yellowtail, each weighing between fifteen and twenty pounds. They ranged from twenty-seven to thirty-six inches long. We had the bulk of the meat canned at a local cannery and the remainder we filleted, freezing part and, with the rest, we had a fish-fry that night to end all fish-fries! Fish from the market never tasted like that; our skills as fishermen, no doubt.

Through the summer, while launching the "Rock 'n Row" at Dana Landing, Grandpa Jim and Gene spotted a poor, sad boat that looked as if nobody loved it. Its broken windows and peeling paint greatly intriguing these three Men of the Sea. This boat was about 25 feet long and had a Chrysler Marine engine, visible thanks to missing floorboards. That was about all that could be seen because the cabin was locked-up tight. The fellows admired the lines of the boat and shamed the owner for his neglect. Then, before we knew it, the summer was over and the fishing season was put away to get ready for the Christmas holidays. This takes some serious getting ready when a family is so fortunate as to have four small boys.

The Log – Part 2

As each season must, Christmas passed. On a Sunday ride early in the new year, we just happened by Dana Landing and there it was! Jim spotted that same sad boat we'd seen at the close of the last fishing season, now lying on its side on the beach behind the boathouse. We just had to park the car and walk down to look her over. All we could see was lots of work that needed to be done.

When we got home, Jim began to pace the floor, vowing he would not call about it. He said it would just mean trouble for him. So, I called. The boat was for sale. "I'll give you a good price," the man said, "because of the work that needs to be done." Boy! The work that needed to be done! Well, whether it was telepathy or whatever, Grandpa called right after I hung up the phone. I told him about our new "discovery."

The Scott-Atwater partnership had by this time been dissolved due to the financial pressures of raising small boys and going to college and now any boat buying was strictly up to Grandpa. Even without funds, one and all we were able to give advice and comments, and one thing we all agreed on, except Nonie, was that we "Needed" that boat. Nonie, being a heart patient, wouldn't go anywhere on anything unless she could rest. Naively, Grandpa thought a bunk and a "head" and a rigged pole ought to make ours the happiest Nonie ever. So, down they came to investigate.

In force, we went to Dana Landing and found the boat still wallowing around in the tides. The owner unlocked the cabin for us and for several happy hours we swarmed over her like bees. A "sturdy seaworthy vessel" this with a bilge full to prove it; windows but no glass; paint peeling off; and an engine that won't run–but don't despair: two bunks she boasts and a "head" that works, so all is not lost.

After a week of thinking (dreaming) and looking and dickering, we were launched again! Amid cheers and tears, we saw our boat floated out in the bay, and another boat tow it out of the small harbor and into the open sea for a short cruise around Point Loma and into the main San Diego harbor to be dry-docked. We drove to Cabrillo National Monument at the end of Point Loma from where, high above the sea, the view of the Pacific Ocean on one side and San Diego Harbor on the other is breathtaking. The sun was shining on a calm blue sea and we even spotted a grey whale off the point on its way to Baja California and the calving grounds. We watched through binoculars as our little boat bobbed along on that big ocean, around the point and down the channel of San Diego Bay. Past anchored Navy ships and cruising outboards, she was towed like the best of them. We were all filled with happiness as we watched our boat pulled up on the dolly and dry-docked. Nonie watched the whole operation until she had to retreat to a couch where she conceded at last: "We need this boat!"

The Log – Part 3

Once more, Ernie and I sorted kids while the sea-going gentlemen of the family went to work on the boat. The first operation was to clean the bilge. "Clean the bilge" sounded something like "vacuum the hall" but grease and muck and slop that had to be scraped off, loaded in buckets, and dumped was the order of the day and what a detail this turned out to be.

All Saturday afternoon and evening and from sun-up Sunday, the boys "cleaned the bilge." For the money they had never worked so hard. With "Joy-water" as they called it, they scrubbed the bilge with brushes until all the hide came off their knuckles and they had permanent kinks in their spines. Pretty soon (though not soon enough) it was Sunday night again and the four tired adults loaded one rusty, beat-up looking boat engine on a trailer, two small sleepy boys and numerous sundries in the car, and back home they went.

Our little house quivered for a while, but soon everything was back in order and we were making plans for the next weekend which, I might add, turned out to be a corker!

⚓ ⚓ ⚓

Lending a Hand with the Cleanup

The following Friday, Nonie and Grandpa arrived at 9:30 p.m. with groceries, power saws, pajama shirts (but no bottoms), and one toothbrush between them. We prepared to work. As we all know, the best-laid plans of mice and men – and all that sort of thing; things don't always go as planned. In this case, as we discovered by Sunday night, our only trouble was too many planners.

Jim planned to sand and scrape the bottom. Gene planned to glass the decks, so he brought a "kit" and proceeded. The Allisons, Ernie's parents, also from Riverside, had arrived Saturday morning bringing Gene and Ernie, Mike and Tim, and fourteen-year-old "Aunt" Peg. The Allisons planned to sleep in their little fourteen-foot house trailer which had also made the trip to San Diego.

Mr. Allison had kindly come to lend his carpenter's skills and he had "planned" to build a new flying bridge. I'm not sure what Grandpa "planned" to do but I am sure it didn't matter because, with all the other plans, he didn't need any of his own anyway.

One small factor no one had reckoned with was the weather. To say it rained was the understatement of the year, but not until the boat was ripped apart at the seams, sanded here and there, and the "fiberglassing" begun. Fiberglassing is a process that is better done, if at all, by experts or on a warm sunny day so the resin will dry quickly. Neither being the case, we had quite a different effect than "planned." Resin "icicles" hung down the sides and big round bubbles covered the deck. By Sunday morning, everyone had given up the weekend and Grandpa got brushes and sal-soda and started after the head or 'John" as we fondly called it (Grandpa's parents named him John) and which had been brought home to be cleaned.

Gee Whiz Being Lifted Out of the Water for Servicing

When the Allisons came in from sleeping in their trailer Sunday morning, they looked like wet cats; the trailer had leaked all night and they had been thoroughly miserable. The children thought it more fun to fight than play since they had so many anxious referees and in all the confusion of eight adults and five children counting Aunt Peg. In that small two-bedroom house, with rain pounding at the windows and running on the porch, who could blame them. One can't "paste pictures" forever.

During one of the "battles," Poor Grandpa got a bottle of applesauce dropped on him. While it was running down his face and Nonie was mopping at his sweater, he announced, "Some days it just doesn't pay to get up."

For some reason, this touched my "funny bone," maybe because I was responsible for dropping the applesauce, but the whole weekend seemed like a gigantic joke the fates played on all of us. Since the comedy had been endemic ever since this boat adventure had begun, it all seemed part of the game.

Everyone went home early that Sunday and, as before, we began to plan for the next weekend.

We had all been considering lofty highhanded names for the boat and everyone had submitted his favorite, but on this particular weekend and many others which followed, the comment "Gee Whiz!" seemed pretty standard in our customary conversation. Appropriate on so many occasions, even the children used it.

Preparing the Newly Named *Gee Whiz*

We didn't know much about rebuilding boats, and the expense of "dry storage," brass screws, and marine paint. Soon Grandpa and Nonie began to have an expression on their faces that looked like "Gee Whiz!"

Well, as you can no doubt guess, we began referring to the boat as "Gee Whiz" and one Saturday when the white paint on the stern was almost dry, we found Grandpa perched on a ladder with a mouthful of brass nails and a hand full of brass letters and when he was finished, we all stood back in our paint and resin-smeared clothes and looked with pride at our *Gee Whiz*.

⚓ ⚓ ⚓

The Newly Refinished *Gee Whiz* Going Back into the Water

⚓ ⚓ ⚓

Our "weekends" continued for about three months and scoffed all the money we had. About the time Nonie, Ernie, and I began looking wild-eyed when money was mentioned, the day arrived when back on the cradle our little *Gee Whiz* went. Amid the cheers of the entire family (to say nothing of the employees of *Shelter Island Yacht Ways*) back down the ways she glided. She looked to us more like a $200,000 yacht than any other motorboat in the ways.

Her engine wouldn't run yet but anyone knew how well it would—eventually. It was a very demanding job for the gals to stay at home with the four little men while the three big ones stayed on the boat until 10:00 or 11:00 on Friday and Saturday nights to, in their words, "put 'er in running order."

On the second Sunday after the boat was in the water and tied up to the dock, the "boat widows and orphans" took lunch down to our mechanics. Just as we started down the dock with the repast, we heard an engine cough and sputter and, low and behold, our engine was running. We were thrilled!

After some coaxing, we took the *Gee Whiz* on a very short three laps around the bay. Grandpa was helmsman first. Jim was next and Gene was lucky enough to be at the helm when suddenly water began shooting straight up out of the engine and then the poor Gee Whiz engine just died.

Ernie, with her healthy respect (fear) for the water, grabbed life preservers and kids flew in all directions. Panic reigned unchecked for a few minutes. It seems a minor mistake was made in our hookup and there, not 100 feet from the dock, we dropped our anchor and the three Captains proceeded to right their mistake.

One fishing boat coming in stopped to ask if we needed help. I suppose we were quite a sight; within swimming (or walking) distance of the dock, anchored, and in life jackets. That hour on board is the longest one I have spent so far. All ended well, however, and we began to plan our trip out of Shelter Island and around Pt. Loma and up the coast the fifteen miles to Mission Bay and Santa Clara Pt. where we owned a buoy to which we planned to moor.

The Log – Part Four

At first, we contemplated the three men taking the boat around while the mothers and children remained on dry land, however, this contemplation didn't last long. We decided to do it up right and all ten of us would go. Then we decided that wasn't quite fair either, so the Allisons were invited to go too. Charlene, Ernie's mother, who, to put it mildly, has no sea legs, was game to go despite herself. So, the thirteen of us planned a fried chicken lunch and embarked on the greatest adventure of our lives.

The day arrived cold and foggy with a rough sea. Jim, who had been taking a course from the United States Power Squadron and thought he knew "Port" from "Starboard", endeavored to guide us out of the San Diego harbor. Just in case, we tied our fourteen-foot outboard, *Rock 'n Row*, on behind and away we chugged. The sea was rough, and everyone grew more apprehensive because as we were going out, it seemed everyone else was coming in. We stopped for bait and after several passes at the bait barge, we tied up and the little boys' eyes grew round with wonder as the attendant dropped nets of squirming, wriggling anchovies into our bait tank and all over the cockpit as well. Greg hastened to gather them up with the admonition, "Come here you 'ittle debils."

⚓ ⚓ ⚓

Greg with a Garibaldi

We debated whether to continue because of the fog but decided we were halfway already and bravely we plowed on, around the foghorn and light house, and into the open sea. Everyone lived in a world of his own, even squeezed thirteen together. The sea has a way of making one alone, even among many. Poor Charlene, in her agony of sea sickness, was more alone than the rest and nothing seemed to help her, Dramamine or bunks. Dry land seemed her only salvation.

Ernie and I, determined to serve the lunch, braced ourselves in the cabin, and attempted to serve plates for everyone. No one seemed particularly surprised when they found the fried chicken under the baked beans or their bun filled with potato salad. By this time everyone was prepared for the unusual.

⚓ ⚓ ⚓

Finally, Mission Bay came into view and we headed for the channel. The mouth of this channel can be very rough at certain times since it has been dredged deep and the sea enters as mall passage almost at right angles. The swells were huge and all of us were wide eyed.

Just as we passed the end of the breakwater, our engine coughed and died. We hastily dropped our anchor and once more, up came the floorboard sand three "behinds", as three great heads got together to coax and cajole their "baby" to run again. Their magic touch was in effect and, to our great relief, it started right away and without further ado we were off again.

As we came into the bay itself, the fog seemed to lift, and motorboats and skiers were everywhere. This was bad enough because our Captains were a "team" of novices; however, sailboats, having the right-of-way over motorboats like ours, almost proved our undoing.

Our boat, being heavy and large in comparison with small sailing craft, was hard to maneuver in close quarters and could do considerable damage. Skiers cut in front of us waving merrily and poor Grandpa would throw us into reverse and "wham" the Rock 'n Row still being towed, would ram us in the stern.

We finally got to Santa Clara Point and about 100 feet from the buoy the engine died again and since this particular spot is rather shallow and narrow and wind was blowing, our bow was very quickly aground and Jim, poor soul, happened to be at the helm, a fact he'll never outlive I fear. Gene got in the *Rock 'n Row* and started that lovely big Scott-Atwater motor and pulled us free.

We tied those darn boats up and went home. We were all so tired we didn't say much that evening but at six o'clock the next morning we were aboard again waiting for the fog to lift so we could go back to sea.

The Log – Part Five

Each of us packed many priceless memories into the following weekends. As a family hobby, there is just nothing like boating. For the children these were grand experiences, but I believe they were even more grand for the adults. We seemed to learn more about each other, and a family bond grew between us that had never been there so strong before.

The mooring buoy at Santa Clara Point didn't prove too satisfactory for us because we Jim throwing an anchor overboard. used our boat every weekend from Friday 'till Sunday and having to row out and bring her into the dock was a nuisance so we rented a slip, #113 at Mission Bay Yacht Landing, and moved our pride and joy to new lodgings.

We spent all our leisure time at that landing because it was so convenient and such fun. We spent hours watching other boating enthusiasts all around, enjoying who could tell the tallest fish *tail*; tale that is.

Boats of all sizes and descriptions can be found here, from lovely big yachts to 12-foot outboards. Nonie and the children spent most of their time lying on the cabin top in the sunshine and watching the world go by and regularly making a fresh pot of coffee. Grandpa "worked on the boat."

As soon as Grandpa's knuckles would heal, another weekend would roll around and he would soon fix that condition. Almost everyone we knew was invited to share our pleasure. Grandpa was very democratic about the whole thing. He took everyone in the company where he worked fishing, from the president and his entire family to the janitor and his wife. Everyone went home from the trip uttering the same phrase, "Boy, this is the way to live!" We roamed from La Jolla coves to the tip of Pt. Loma and often to the Coronado Islands every weekend in search of Yellowtail. The first one caught will be the last one forgotten.

Gary Proudly Displays His First Small Catch for the Season

Grandpa, Jim, and Gary went out one afternoon while Nonie and I stayed home and washed our hair and babysat Greg. They trolled up and down from the channel to La Jolla and on the last trip along about Crystal Pier in Pacific Beach, Gary gave his famous, "Hook-Up!" yell. Grandpa slowed down the old *Gee Whiz* expecting to land another barracuda, but this little old fish had more fight than an average barracuda, almost more fight than Gary could manage.

Gary reeled and fought and when his arms ached from holding that busy pole, Jim would hold the weight of it for just a second, because that's all the longer Gary could stand for someone else to hold his fish. Jim shouted directions 'til his voice gave out and finally, there below in that green ocean was a magnificent Yellowtail. When Grandpa gaffed him and he was aboard, Gary was so excited his big blue eyes filled up with tears and he said, "Gee Whiz!" The three fishermen headed straight home, this was big doings and had to be shared. We were waiting for them on the dock when they came in but while the boat was still way out in the channel, we could hear Jim yelling "Gary got a Yellowtail! Gary got a Yellowtail!"

Everyone around seemed to think we were nuts. They paid little attention to this proud father dancing around on the bow of a boat and croaking in an all-gone voice. That was a most happy day and one we'll never forget.

Jim carried the fish (like a baby) wrapped in newspaper, up to the scales, telling everyone who'd listen, "My **kid** caught this!" The fish weighed sixteen pounds cleaned and was the top catch on the *Gee Whiz* so far.

The Log — Part Six

Grandpa is the star of the following drama. All I can say is he scared the rest of us out of ten years' growth with this little episode.

In the spring we all took a weeklong vacation, canceled all our appointments with the civilized world, gathered our gear, and went to sea. Along with Grandpa's gear was a bright and beautiful new pole and reel and line that Santa Claus had brought him. He tenderly carried this aboard with sundry leaders, hooks, lures and floats and mentally weighed his catches with this beauty during the ensuing week.

The first day out was something to remember. We fished along Pt. Loma kelp beds on a calm clear sea and caught lots of kelp bass ranging in length from ten inches to two feet. We did a lot of relaxing and soaking up the salt air. We carry lounge pads on the cabin top, and it is one real fine place to nap. We had dinner aboard and along about sunset we just drifted across the kelp for one of the most breath-taking experiences ever.

The sea was so clear we could see the kelp growing and swaying with the current. It was like a wonderland, so quiet and schools of tiny little sea bass darted around the kelp hiding from the larger fish. Small shellfish covered some of the kelp leaves and I was reminded of |ack's Beanstalk as the kelp gave the illusion of one's being able to climb down its broad leaves to the bottom of the sea. I've never seen the water so clear.

We were all hanging over the side of the boat, lost in our own thoughts and the beauties the sea revealed to us. The following day we were back on the boat and Nonie and I scrambled eggs with ham while the Captain and his crew took us out to catch a whale. We fished the morning through without any colossal luck and shortly after lunch I crawled up on the top bunk to snooze awhile.

Well! Suddenly Gary stuck his head in the cabin. It sounded like he screamed, "Mama, Greg's overboard!" Greg being just four and an ardent fisherman but not much of a swimmer, I came out of that bunk awake and on deck in one long leap.

When I landed, Jim and Nonie were pulling a poor, wet, half-hysterical Grandpa aboard as his yachting cap and one shoe floated by on their way to anywhere, and as I counted noses and realized everyone was on deck, I was so relieved it wasn't Greg that it took me awhile to realize what was going on. Grandpa sat on the rail around the cockpit and dripped piteously as he told us a most sorrowful tale. We all thought the poor guy had fallen in, pole and all, because he kept saying, "My pole, I lost my pole." Nonie soothingly said, "It's alright dear. It's all right. You're safe, that's all that matters."

Grandpa's impassioned rejoinder was, "Oh Hell! I dropped my pole and reel and everything and I dived in after it. By God, I almost had it when my glasses went floating by. I thought, uh oh, $60 is a lot so I went after them and damn it, I lost 'em both and had to come up for air."

At this, he reached into his shirt pocket for a cigarette and seemed quite surprised to find them wet as sop. He let out another oath and the children stood by wide eyed while he took off a wet and dripping watch and Nonie tried desperately to dry the vacation money out of a soppy wallet. Jim got out the grappling hook and extra line and tried to snag the pole. According to the chart, we were over a ledge that dropped off about 134 fathoms (804 feet), so the chances of retrieval were slim to nothing.

Grandpa decided if he couldn't get his pole, the least he could save would be his cap and shoe. We pulled up anchor and chugged away looking for a bobbing hat and one lonesome shoe. We finally gave this up as well and threw the other shoe over.

We half-heartedly fished the rest of the day, but to use an old cliche, this little episode took all the wind out of our sails.

Grandpa clammed-up and although plied with many questions, he acted as though he was telling someone else's experience. Gary wanted to know if he noticed the bottom of the boat as he came up and Jim wanted to know how he happened to drop his pole. Nonie firmly believed he fell in and wouldn't admit it. The young Greg asked a very logical question. He queried seriously, "Grandpa, why did you go swimming in your clothes and put your bathing suit on when you got out?"

We were all provoked because we had been so frightened. Even so, I couldn't help feeling sorry for poor Grandpa. He was so sad over the loss of his prized possession.

Just like a child who knows he has been naughty and is sorry, he took all our scolding and ribbing and never said a word. Finally, Gary ardently rebuked, "Okay, let's stop reminding him now!"

As adults, I guess we felt a little ashamed of all relentless chastising Anyway, Grandpa got some quiet and a rest.

The Log – Part Seven

On one happy weekend soon after this scary episode, Gene, Ernie and their boys came with Nonie and Grandpa to do some fishing. Saturday sunup saw us maneuvering alongside the bait shack. When we had secured a line and the attendant looked at us expectantly, Greg said, "We want some bait, but don't give us any old dead ones."

I shuddered and went into the cabin away from that fresh kid. We got not only live ones, but an extra scoop of sardines and a sarcastic wish from the attendant for "good fishing." A real good disposition this man had.

We proceeded out the channel and down towards Pt. Loma, stopping in reverence where Grandpa's pole lay buried.

Gene was elected to toss over the anchor. After pondering our location a while, we chose a likely looking spot. And so, Gene tossed away!

It seems that the line on the anchor was not secured and there went our anchor and 200 feet of new line. The look on Gene's face was something to see. He contemplated going over but thought better of it. Someone yelled, "There went $50 for nothing." Poor Ernie lost her breakfast. She was sick off and on the rest of the day and we all kidded her about being so money mad.

We did get a nice catch of fish for a fry that night and took poor Ernie home. That evening somebody was talking to Tiny Tim and he announced he was "gonna get a bebe," so we all got in on the secret. It took more than $50 to make Ernie "seasick."

Jim Throwing Out the Anchor

Gene generously wrote out a check and said, "Here, Nonie, is my half of the anchor." Nonie said, "Hey, where do I go to buy half an anchor?"

To relieve everyone's angst, good old Grandpa and his friends at the welding shop concocted an anchor of their own. You can darn well bet all lines were secured from then on when the old *Gee Whiz* was anchored.

Since Ernie had spent such a miserable Saturday, she and I stayed home Sunday and the rest of the family went with Gene to catch a Yellowtail. He fought that fish for ten minutes and then the line went slack and he said he'd lost it, so he began to reel it in, but it was pretty hard reeling.

About this time, Jim's line became fouled and they had quite a time. It seems Jim's line crossed Gene's when Jim was trying to reel in out of the way and it took the pressure off. Gene thought he'd lost his fish.

The boat was going slow all this time but with those too reeling as fast as possible. They finally reeled in and found a dead Yellowtail on Gene's line. They had pulled it through the water until they'd drowned it! No wonder it quit fighting!

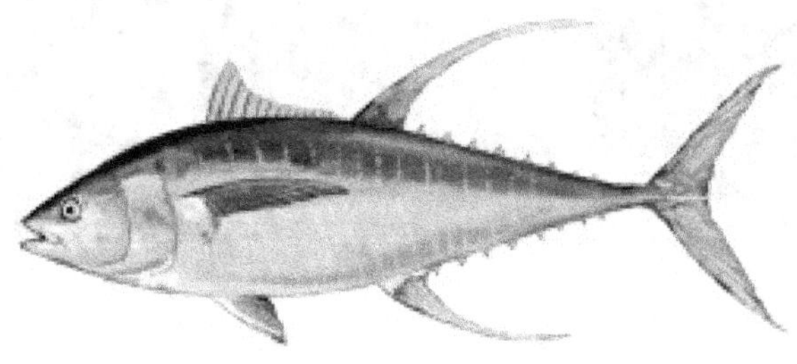

Giant Yellowtail

The Log – Part Eight

Towards the end of the summer, Grandpa and Nonie managed a few days off and came down to make one last try for a Yellowtail for Grandpa since, on his own boat, he'd caught everything but a Yellowtail. One certain Wednesday morning, Nonie, Grandpa, Gary, Greg, and I decided to go out and give it a try. Everyone else was working.

There had been a bad storm off Baja California over the previous weekend, but we didn't worry about it then. At this time there was a dredge working in the channel not too far from the mouth and just as we passed the dredge, we noticed an outboard, about a sixteen-footer, riding the crest of what seemed to be an unusually large ground swell.

Coming into Shelter Island for Repair

What particularly made us take notice was the skipper who was standing up, hanging on to the wheel with both hands and his terrified expression was directed dead ahead. Not more than one ground swell past him and our expression was terrified too! The little boys of course had their life jackets on, but I sat them on preserver cushions on the deck and I was so scared I couldn't even think straight.

When one swell would pass under our stem the bow would be on thin air, at least eight feet of it. As the bow would dip down water would fly all over us. Greg yelled, "Mama, look at the water mountain!" Until this time, Jim and I had been busy watching where we were going but as I looked aft, I saw what really looked like a water mountain.

In the cabin, meanwhile, cups were flying everywhere. The top of the sugar bowl came unscrewed and cube sugar flying around just like bullets from a machine gun. Maybe to an old salt these ground swells wouldn't have been too bad, but to a novice like me, with two children and a heart patient on board, they were worse than bad—they were horrible.

Well, here Grandpa starred again. He kept a very level head and took time taking us out of the channel, heading dead on into the swells, and as soon as he could safely, he turned around and we went in again. The hell with Yellowtail!

All of us were so glad to see slip #113 we could have kissed it. The little boys wanted to know what we'd forgotten and why we'd come in so soon. They thanked Grandpa for a nice boat ride but Nonie nor I had anything to say. We laid around in the sun all afternoon and had dinner on board. As usual Grandpa was playing "bottoms-up" with that mysterious engine.

The next day, Jim and Grandpa were just talking and Grandpa said he thought he would sell the "Gee Whiz" and get a smaller boat he could handle alone more easily. Nonie was lying around half asleep but at overhearing this she was suddenly very much awake.

"That's what you think. After yesterday, the next one is going to be at least the size of the *Seabiscuit*. The very idea, a smaller one!" Then back to her nap she went. The *Seabiscuit* is a 50' commercial sportfisher with a very able captain who is affectionately called "Chili." Nonie's statement was made before she heard that on the same day she spoke of, the *Seabiscuit* had been out and had taken a wave clear over her! Oh well. I guess the next boat will have to rival the *Queen Mary*.

The Log – Part Nine

By now fall was in the air and school for two little boys this year, Gury and Mike. So, the boat saw us fewer weekends and soon hardly at all because once again we had to help Santa Claus get ready for the big day of the year. Besides, one of the spokes in our wheel was missing; our lady in waiting could no longer fit into her sea pants After a lovely holiday and a very happy New Year, a lovely little pearl was added to our treasure chest. Ernie called her Kimberly Beth and she made our family circle truly complete. As Mike put it, "we sure did need a girl-type!"

This time Gene and Ernie weren't with us. They were saving their trips for work. Shelter Island Yacht Ways seemed very glad to see us and once again were very hospitable. We were more cautious this time and I guess quieter. Within three weeks Nonie had painted everything, including Grandpa's sweater, and Grandpa and Gene had worked over the engine, enlarged the rudder and fixed a leaky packing around the exhaust. With a new coat of bottom paint, she was ready for the water again and another year of fishing.

The colossal invoice from Shelter Island made us glad to leave. As result of the shocking bill, Grandpa was kinda blue. He forlornly mumbled, "I guess we'll just sell 'er."

He and Gene took her back around Pt. Loma to Mission Bay and the trip was lovely. The old sea was smooth as glass and sang a siren's song. Grandpa grinned and said, "It's really a shame to sell her now. She's in such good condition. Let's wait until we've had at least a few more good trips." As we walked off the dock, a passer-by pointed at the *Gee Whiz* and exclaimed, "Boy, that's the kind of boat to have!"

And by golly, **he was right!**

"Delivery" – Pop in Charge

"Pome" for Pop

He pulled his cap down almost to his chin,
But through his stern look came the trace of a grin.
He started the engine and cast off the line,
Looked at the weather and then at the time.
The rain didn't matter, he headed for sea,
The sun in his pocket to be hung when he pleased.
The salty sea spray was a Siren's beckon,
And the the engines "thumpata" a gamble he'd recon
He'd played "bottoms-up" before, that's for sure,
So he guessed once more he could surely endure.
He readied a line and got out a jig,
And threw them both over. (WHAT HE'S AFTER IS BIG.)
He fished all that day for a fish or a lark,
He wandered alone through waves deep and dark.
Tben. finally turned the bow towards the shore,
On this day at least, he'd wander no more.
He plowed through colors from blue to pale green
And wondered about all the things that he'd seen.
He rolled up his line and shrugged off the jig,
(THAT FISH MUST HAVE REALLY BEEN BIG.)
What he got from the sea only his heart knew for certain,
But there on the shore was a light and a curtain
And faces all anxiously straining to see
The bow of his boat coming home from the sea.

—Joy

The End

Debut

A very young couple knocked on the door of a small cottage that sat back a long way from the dirt road. In tears the pregnant young woman asked if she could come home to have her baby. My wonderful, loving and Christian Grandmother said, "Of course, my Darling," and so it was that I was delivered into her strong and capable hands the next afternoon about 1:00 p.m.

The spirit of my Grandmother is like a thread of gold woven throughout the fabric of my life. Her influence on her family and her friends never ended. She was a small Irish lady, one of many children born to a Baptist minister and his wife. She stubbornly refused their religion until she was sixteen. According to her, when the Lord chose to, he took her heart and soul-forever. She lived what she believed every day of her life and I have no doubt she is dressed in robes of white and is still doing THE LORD'S WORK.

When she was eighteen, she was greeted by my future Grandfather, David. He was an orphan and the promised beau of my Grandmother's older sister. He came riding into town again because it was time to take a wife. (Grandmother's older sister he assumed.) The older sister had married years ago and had moved away with her husband. David had been away three years and had no idea the older sister was unavailable. After all, there weren't too many electronic forms of communication in the eighteenth century.

Well, Grandmother said that was her lucky day. She went right to work to heal his broken heart. Her Irish blue eyes sparkled as she told how she had loved him from around the corner all the days he had been courting her sister. They were married by her Father soon after this encounter. Ultimately, they had thirteen children together.

They brought their large family to California and it was here my Mother, their twelfth child, was born in Imperial County. My Grandfather was a farmer by trade and a good one. Times got very hard for farmers during the Great Depression. When my Grandfather heard the oilfields in Orange County needed workers, they went in a covered wagon and camped out like thousands of others looking for new opportunity. With three growing sons to help, they soon had a home again. Everyone worked together. And all the family stayed in and around Orange County as they started their own lives.

Grandmother was the heart of the family. Recreation was music. We all gathered and sang while one aunt played the piano. one the harmonica, two uncles on guitars, and everyone singing. Saturday night was grand. All the little ones sat around Grandmother and clapped their hands in time. It didn't take long before even the smallest one of us could sing hymns. That wasn't all that was sung, however. One of my favorite other tunes is still "*When Irish Eyes Are Smiling.*"

And could we ever harmonize. One exultant Thanksgiving, with more than thirty people together, there was no more space to put the food. The dining table stretched through the dining room and the bedroom. When room ran out, four pumpkin pies were placed on the foot of my Grandmother's bed, with its grand white coverlet. An extra tablecloth carefully covered them until dessert time.

Before dinner, Aunt Lola was telling an important story about some of the crazy things that happened at her restaurant and decided to sit down on the bed to finish the tale. We were all laughing so hard about her story, we forgot about the pies. She sat square in the middle of the bed. The splat of the pie was unmistakable!

We managed to recover the remaining pies. The white bedspread somehow became white again. Anything belonging to Grandmother eventually seemed to return to pristine condition. Her wooden drain-board was kept snow white. The floors were scrubbed white. Her hair was white and very long, and on special occasions she allowed small hands to brush, braid and adorn it.

Grandma also had a wonderful garden which we inspected together early in the mornings when I was lucky enough to be there. She made rhubarb sauce that was pink and sweet; homemade biscuits three inches high, with golden tops and soft delicious insides; sauerkraut from home grown cabbages; new potatoes cooked with fresh green beans; corn on the cob dripping with homemade butter; and every kind of jam you could want for the biscuits.

Summer was a time for canning. All those beautiful canned foods were stored in polished mason jars on perfectly stocked shelves in the service room. Shelves that reached from floor to ceiling. On March 10, 1933 at 5:20 p.m. an earthquake hit the Long Beach area of Southern California that measured 6.3 on the Richter scale. All the mason jars in the service room came crashing down to the floor which wasn't in great condition itself. Glass was everywhere.

The shaking earth was predicted to continue into the evening. Everyone slept in their cars that night. The next morning a neighbor came over to rescue my Grandmother who was singing praises at the top of her lungs while she shoveled jam into a washtub. She wasn't afraid and wouldn't leave what she was about. The neighbor went away shaking his head, and saying, "Ah well, it takes more than an earthquake to shake up Mother Ralston!" She was singing *"Amazing Grace"* and soon was joined by neighbors who could hear her song. Her faith in her Lord never wavered, even when later she suffered a paralyzing stroke.

For the most part Grandma's prayers were silent, except for her singing. The first time I saw her "SHOUT," I was still a child. This first SHOUTING was a lot like the last time I saw the SHOUTING transpire shortly after her stroke.

The stroke left her with paralysis on her left side, and this affected her hands as well as her feet. She explained, "SHOUTING about The Lord loving me so much sends His Holy Spirit to fill my soul to overflowing!" And she would begin to clap her hands faster than imaginable, and her face would be transfixed with total Joy. Tears would stream down her face and she seemingly saw something no one else could see.

On a notable SHOUTING right after her stroke the seeming possession lasted thirty to forty seconds. After being paralyzed from the stroke, seeing her begin to clap spiritedly during this time was wondrous. After that, she could use her hand, but always used a crutch to walk.

She died the summer after her stroke. Even though she had not been able to attend church for many years prior, the congregation in the church was overflowing for the memorial service. I felt grief only for myself because I missed her. For her, I could only rejoice. She was where she wanted to be: Home with her Lord.

Twice since her death she has come to me. The first time was shortly after the birth of my first son. She had been concerned about it before her death. Gary arrived in the world at 1:17 in the morning on the fifth day of May. Thinking I would never have children, I thought he was a true miracle.

I was so ecstatic that when I was finally back in my room at 3:3O A.M., I couldn't sleep. I was saying a prayer of Thanksgiving when suddenly the breeze stirred the curtain of the third-story window and I saw my Grandmother standing beside my bed. She smiled at me and then was gone.

The second time she appeared was thirty years later. Unlike my Grandmother, my faith had wavered. Life had been difficult. I had become despondent and did not want to live.

Onc night alone in my apartment, I had a dream. In this dream I heard my voice called over and over and went to see what it was. Suddenly I realized I was not on my bed. Instead I could see my body lying on the bed and I heard a gathering of several relatives in another room. They were in mourning. I heard my distraught Grandmother, who kept repeating, "No. No. No. ..."

I turned to follow a sound I heard, eerie and sort of electronic. It seemed to be approaching me along with a very strong white light. I can remember wandering, as if it would be too painful to pass through the curtain. In an instant, the sound eased, and the light stopped, and I heard a voice ask me, "WHY DO YOU HESITATE?"

My answer, much to my surprise, was , "I want to know my grandchild." The light receded and the noise stopped. My mourning relatives were all gone. I awoke and was ice cold. I was no longer in doubt that I wanted to live. I have never known such peace as I felt for several months following.

A beautiful baby girl was born to Gary and his wife a few months later. Not only is named for me, she truly is a Joy in my life.

My Grandmother would say, "The Lord works in mysterious ways, His wonders to perform!"

A Lady on the Skids

She lay wallowing in the tide, turned on her side, her bottom bared tor all the world to see. A lady on the skids, you might say. Having great compassion, and little good sense, John couldn't walk away. This old boat was twenty-five-feet long, and at least that many years old. Her paint was ragged, and her bilge was filled to capacity. The Chrysler engine hidden beneath the deck was a rusty, ignominious piece of machinery, a challenge to any good junk dealer.

Of course, even a lady on the skids has some virtues; sometimes they must he carefully sought out. It took John about three months and two- thousand dollars to find the virtues that were so carefully and well-hidden in the framework of this "lady".

The restoration of antique furniture is a hobby that is practiced more and more in our society. Some sociologists tie this to the lack of ancestral ties in America. Perhaps it's their desire for prestige end solidarity in good and lasting things that have survived the years. Other sociologists seem to think it reflects more our fear of the future, and therefore our reaching towards the past.

A boat can't be classed as furniture, but somehow, somewhere, there must be a reason to cause a man to work harder for nothing than he would work on any job, for any amount of money. The chances for success were overwhelmingly against him. In the first place. to anyone but a madman, restoration of the wretched hull looked impossible. He bought it for one-thousand dollars cash.

He first had the bilge pumped dry and the boat floated free of the sand. It was towed to dry-dock, and with the help of friends and family. John did most of the work himself. For a month, while the work was feverishly in progress, the weather refused to have any part part in the whole affair and threw a real damper on the whole development with two inches of rain to make progress almost hopeless.

If the flame of enthusiasm could have been turned to "simmer" until the weather was agreeable, things might not have been so bad. Unfortunately, the boat was purchased in January, and the fishing season begins in late April, and the heat was on "high." John and his crew of helpers, scraped the bilge free of a lifetime accumulation of grease, fish scales, and various fishing hooks. Everything that could come loose was hauled out for repair. Some things that came loose shouldn't have, but on the other hand, some things we added that hadn't been there before. All in all, it balanced out pretty well. A new fiberglassed bottom replaced the bore-worm infested skeg, and a new canopy replaced the old windshield.

The old boat was propped up on barrels, her deck being some eight to ten feet off the ground. Ladders leaned against her sides, end canvas sheets lay below John's most willing workers were his son, Jack, and his son-in-law, Jim. (They expected to get a lot of free fishing out of the deal.)

John made most use of the ladders. Jack and Jim got to use the canvas to lie on in order to sand off the bottom paint. Sanding is a messy job anyway you look at it, but from their angle, it was insufferable. Sanding was bad enough, but the plan hadn't reckoned with bottom paint. Jack and Jim made the mistake of thinking this was the paint on the bottom of the boat. Not so.

"Bottom paint: A red colored, usually copper paint which has qualities to discourage marine growth." It is known to the seasoned sailor as anti-fouling paint. The "anti" can hardly apply when it comes to the time to sand it off and repaint. "Foul" does.

These two hardy souls wore oxygen masks, complained bitterly, threatened everything (loudly), more like "real sailors" supposedly contend. No amount of precisely directed wrath helped.

The scraping came first. The marine growth apparently didn't know it was supposed to be discouraged. At any rate, it had grown profusely over the years. The sanding had to be done again and again and again... Many coats of paint needed removal. At last, with blossoming rashes from chemicals and marine blight, the would-be fishermen discovered a hull beneath the layers.

Unfortunately, that was not all they discovered. Bore worms had been having regular meals on the backbone (the keel) of the boat. Large sections of the keel had to be removed and replaced. This operation called for skill, patience, and money—and John was running short on the latter two. Even so, only the best materials would do for this "lady," and pricey polished brass, precision bolts, and heavy-duty screws would be used to hold everything together.

Once the hull was reassembled, the next project was fiberglassing. A smelly, messy, and precise chemical process to make the hull watertight. It also depends on clear weather—

because moisture and cold will prevent the fiberglass resin from hardening.

A few sunny days had hovered around, promising spring. The weekend arrived when the fiberglass fabric was cut and properly fitted. With the help of many aching arms, the fabric held to the hull while resin was thickly painted on.

Just as the resin was slathered on, the clouds evolved spritely from cumulus to cumulus-nimbus. Rain menaced. The resin was applied faster and faster. The bottom of the boat was critical and with a little luck the sea breeze could discourage the direction of the nimbus and the operation could be a success.

Once again, weather refused cooperation on the project. A few sprinkles turned into an inch of steady rain. The fiberglass material on one side slide unceremoniously to the ground. The resin-infused fiberglass on the other side looked like it had a bad case of all over mumps. This resin would never harden. The boat didn't look anymore dejected than did the novice shipbuilders. Indeed, the day was sad.

With the coming of the sun the next, however, enthusiasm burned brightly again. The determined fishermen (mentally counting their fish) set about repairing damage. And you guessed it: more sanding, sanding, sanding and then painting, painting, painting...

The newly fiberglassed hull was painted the sparkling white only seen on new boats. The cabin and canopy were painted "sea-breeze" blue and at the top of the boat was one-half inch of striped color connecting the white hull with the red anti-fouling bottom. Inside, the cabin received soothing mixture of the remaining white and blue.

The ultimate painting transpired when the half-filled paint cans from the "shipbuilders" empty garages where thrown together in a large container. The unique mixture of paints became the indescribable bilious color that was slopped over the bilge. By this time, the painters had achieved a rather hysterical condition and they considered the bilge paint job their "masterpiece." Well, it's a private affair really. Thank heavens the floorboards cover it nicely.

At long last, the newly painted and repaired engine was hosted aboard. The barrels were rolled away and the boat went back on the cradle to meet the water. Her skids had been removed and she hardly seemed the same at all. She was quite a "civilized lady" now.

Virtue had won. John was proud.

In a Far Away Place

A Simple Fairy Tale

Once upon a time, in a far-off kingdom, lived a wise old woman who had very pink cheeks, a small rosy mouth, and twinkling blue eyes that saw everything. She wound her long white hair into a knot on top of her head and fastened it there with a tortoise shell comb that was five inches long. She was a wise old woman and knew everything there was to know. At least she thought she did.

One day, late in the year when the leaves are turning gold, Old Knight rode by on a very large brown horse that whinnied and swished his tail a lot. Old Knight was very tired. He had just fought and lost one more battle. His sword was very dulled from being used so much and even had a nick in one side. It hung loosely against the horse and sort of slap-slapped against his side as he walked along. Now old Wise Woman lived all alone with Grey Cat in a marvelous small cottage. Still, she felt very lonely, with just grey cat and herself. She longed for a good companion.

Yellow roses grew all around the little cottage door; they were overgrown and badly needed trimming. Smoke curled from the rock chimney toward the sky because Wise Woman was always baking bread. It smelled so good and the roses were so beautiful.

Old Knight was so tired, he paused on the pathway and wondered if he dared to linger there.

From the window above the table, Wise Woman saw him and smiled her sweet smile. She waited anxiously for him to come to her door, but he didn't. He just looked longingly and rode on down the path. Brown Horse, however, did not want to go on; he held fast to the bit in his mouth and he walked sideways and even began to limp a little.

Old Knight began to feel sorry for Brown Horse and so it was they turned around and went back to the cottage. When Old Knight passed the window the first time, Wise Woman had just shrugged her shoulders and went to check on her bread. She did not see him return. She was startled when she heard a rap-rap-rap on her door.

She closed the oven door and went to see who could be there, the hot pads still in her hands. She was pleased when she saw Old Knight, smiled, and asked the weary traveler to rest and to refresh himself.

Brown Horse smiled too as he found a shed with fresh hay and oats for supper. Old Knight and the big sword were off his back and he felt much better. Old Knight and Wise Woman ate large bowls of stew and fresh bread for supper. Old Knight was hardly finished when his sleepy eyes began to close and his head fell to his chest. He quickly began to snore.

There was just one problem. Old Knight snored SO loud when he slept that he even kept Grey Cat awake. Now Grey Cat very much liked to curl-up into a fur ball and sleep with his motor running. His favorite place to be was in the rocking chair by the fire. Old Knight liked this place best too and every night at half-past eight o'clock, his tummy all full, and his toes all warm, there he'd be.

Grey Cat would fluff her tail in disgust and swish it about, complaining loudly before securing another soft spot to rest upon. Wise Woman watched and waited, wondering each night who would get there first. Of course, you know, it was really her rocking chair and her knitting beside it; but it was so nice having Old Knight there for company.

Old Knight was handy too. He trimmed the yellow rose vines and hoed all the garden. The weeds were all gathered into bundles and the firewood was stacked by the fence. Wise Woman liked her old companion, if only he didn't snore so loudly.

Late one evening when the stars should have been out, the wind began to whistle around the cottage and the door blew open. Old Knight hastened to latch the door tightly, but he noticed a little rain on the wind and feared a storm was coming.

Before morning the thunder began to roll around the cottage and the clouds fell close about and grew very black and ominous. Lightning would crack across the sky and the clouds hid the sun when the morning came. The wind blew the trees over until their tops touched the ground and all the yellow roses blew away and their leaves went with them.

Grey Cat screeched and howled and hid under the big bed in the far corner and would not come out. Smoke came down the chimney and choked everyone. The great storm howled for a mighty long time and all the fences were all blown down. The rain formed small rivulets down the roof, over the windows and along the side of the house. Soon it was a river, carrying dirt and plants and rocks and it swept away the path. The wind blew the door open and forced its way into the house. The shutters blew away and still the storm raged on. The little cottage shuddered and slowly sank into a pile of rubble.

Somehow Old Knight managed to cling to a timber as the river gushed. He climbed on top of the heap and there he rested. The old iron stove lay on its side, torn free from the chimney that had carried all the good bread smells into the air. The oven door creaked a little and Old Knight watched amazed as Wise Woman crawled out of her hiding place and lay on the ground. Her long white hair was all wet and black from soot and her tortoise shell comb was gone. Her eyes were closed. Her face was covered with mud.

Old Knight gently bent over her and just as gently he cleaned her face with his shirt. Her eyes fluttered a little and opened. She smiled up at him. He helped her to stand and they held hands as they surveyed the destruction that was everywhere.

"Oh, woe is me!" moaned the woman. "Never can I build my house again." She covered her face with her hands and began to weep. Old Knight felt very sorry for her. Suddenly he thought about his great Brown Horse that for so long had carried him everywhere. And he remembered his old sword with the nick in its blade and he felt sorry for himself too.

Sitting there for hours pondering their doom, Brown Horse found them. When the fences blew away, Brown Horse had run along with them and he had traveled far. His return was cause for a big celebration. Old Knight and Wise Woman were so glad to see him that everyone laughed and danced. With the help of Brown Horse, the work began. They worked together for days rolling stones together and stacking them to form new walls. The old stove got a new chimney and before long a lovely new cottage made of stones stood in the clearing waiting for the roses to grow again.

On a bright spring day, when the birds were singing, Old Knight was feeling so fine. He noticed his feet were itching and he decided it was time for another ride on Brown Horse. He polished his sword, mounted his horse, tipped his hat, then blew Wise Woman a kiss as he rode down the new path. Wise Woman smiled her shrewd little smile and waved goodbye. She knew he would return another day.

Gone Fishing

Billy got quietly out of bed and reached for his pants. The cold dark morning made him hurry, but his hands were so cold they wouldn't work quite right, and the buttons on his shirt di4 not come out evenly with the buttonholes. The first stop was the kitchen. He stuffed a biscuit and an apple in his coat pocket, pulled his hat down around his ears, and hurried out the door.

The sun was just peeking over the hill and Billy could see the lake. It was a very dark blue, like it was still sleeping. The sleepy lake had one pink spot on it where the sun was teasing sunrise. The boat sat on the bank—pulled up where he and Gran had left it last night. The morning air was so crisp with cold it made Billy shiver. He hunched his shoulders and pulled his neck down inside his jacket. He blew his breath out and watched it turn into steam, then he looked around for Tip.

Tip was standing next to Billy, yawning and stretching—one long leg at a time. Billy whispered, "Come on boy!" and they ran down the path from the cottage to the lake where the boat rested. Tip jumped in the boat, wagged his tail devotedly, and waited for Billy to push out from the shore.

The boat gently rocked back and forth. The water made a wet "slap-slap" sound against the hull. Billy climbed in and used an oar to push against the earth to move the boat away from the shore and out onto the lake. They were floating free in just a second and Billy and Tip were ready for adventure—or at least hoping to catch a fish.

Billy rowed the boat far away from the shore, and by this time the sun was nosing over the tall straight pine trees that adorned the mountain. It made the air a little bit warmer and Billy decided it was time to fish. Fishing was what he liked most. Well, next to Gran's storytelling and the cookies they got at the little store down the mountain.

Billy thought every summer he spent with Gran was the best one yet. He opened the tackle box sitting on the bottom of the boat and rummaged around for the hooks and the bottle of salmon eggs which they used for bait. Mountain trout liked the pink round salmon eggs, and Billy placed one on a small fishhook which he carefully attached to his line as he had been instructed to do.

He picked up the pole from the bottom of the boat and cast carefully over his head, sending the weight far out into the lake. It went plip plop when it landed and little circles formed around the place it fell that kept getting bigger and bigger until finally, they reached the boat. The circles rocked the boat softly back and forth.

"I'm gonna surprise Gran with a fresh-caught trout for breakfast. Won't that be neat?" Tip wagged his tail and laid down in the bottom of the boat. He crossed his paws and patiently put his head down on them. He knew fishing took a lot of waiting, and the best way to wait was to sleep.

The gently rocking boat helped the sleepy feeling. Pretty soon the warm sunshine splashed over the lake and found Billy resting his head on Tip. Both were fast asleep. The fishing pole that Bill still held in his hand, got heavier and heavier until finally it rested against the boat. Suddenly there was a tug on the line that was so BIG it almost pulled the pole out of the boat.

The boat rocked way over on its side and the reel sang out, "Wheeeeeeennnnnnn!" There was the biggest fish you would ever see; Great Big Fish swam away with the bait and the hook and even pulled the boat along behind him.

"Gee Whiz, Tip. This is the biggest fish in the whole wide world. He's taking us to China, maybe. I don't know if I can hold on to him!" Tip barked his approval and stood up. The boat began to rock even worse than it did before and Billy fell, still holding on to the pole and scrambling for a place to sit and hold onto the boat.

All the time the reel was still singing, "Wheeeeeeeennnnnennnnn!" Billy reeled and reeled. Tip barked and barked and jumped and jumped. Billy rolled over, and then over again and this time it was boat and all.

Billy fell smack into the water and down, down, down he went... and where was Tip? He couldn't see Tip anymore. Then all he saw was Great Big Fish that had a Great Big Mouth and that fish opened that Great Big Mouth and he swallowed Billy right up.

Billy tumbled around in all that water with a few small fish and with a final swoosh, he went down into the stomach of the fish. He sat down on a small box he found and tried to catch his breath. He looked around him and tried to decide what he should do now.

"Boy, what would Gran think if she knew where I am." thought Billy. "Gee Whiz. The belly of a fish is not a very good place for anybody. What can I do to get out of here?" Billy thought hard. He had an idea: "I'll see if I can make him cough me up, sort of like I do when Mom gives me something that tickles my throat. That's it, I'll tickle his throat!"

Billy found a small stick Great Big Fish had swallowed earlier and he began to rub it against the inside of Great Big Fish's throat. He made a drawing on Great Big Fish's inside tummy wall and Great Big Fish did not like it one bit. He dived to the bottom of the lake and took a big gulp of water, in it came and Billy had to swim around everything in the belly. Then the water subsided; Billy grabbed his stick and started scratching and tickling again.

Great Big Fish was swimming and swimming—to a far place Billy and Gran had never fished before. Great Big Fish was getting tired of the hurt in his tummy, and he was looking for Mom Fish. She always stayed up by the dam, so that is where he was going. He swam and he swam, finally he had gone as far as he could go. Great Big Fish had grown so big he couldn't go over the dam where his Mom lived. All he could do was call to her from below the dam.

He kept poking his head above water and making his fish noise. He jumped high in the air before he began to swim in a circle. He just continued to swim in circles until finally Mom Fish appeared and asked him, "Why are you acting so strangely? What made you swim so far?" Great Big Fish replied sadly, "I have a hurt in my belly like I have never had before. Only a Mama could tell me what to do, so I came to see you.· Please, Mama, tell me what to do!" Mom Fish pondered a moment and then quickly replied, "Hold your breath and count to ten, and soon you will be well again!" She swam away with no pretense.

Great Big Fish felt disappointed, but he began to hold his breath and while counting, he began to swim towards the shore. Before he ever got to ten, maybe it was only seven or eight, he felt a sneeze coming on. It was the biggest sneeze you ever heard.

"KERCHOOOOOO!!!!!!!" And what do you think happened? Up came Billy. He flew out of Great Big Fish's mouth—up, up and over the trees and out into the forest he went. He finally landed right on a pine bough, which really wasn't such a bad place to land, except it was way up high in the top of a very tall pine tree.

Billy just laid there for a while and rested. The bough was swaying in the wind a little. All the trees sounded like they were humming a sweet song. The breeze was soft singing. Although entranced by the music, Billy finally decided he should get down. When he looked down, he discovered he was so high up in Great Big Pine Tree that he could see far out over the mountains in many directions. He could even see the lake, but he couldn't see Gran's house no matter how hard he looked.

While he was squinting his eyes and shading them with his hand and searching for Gran's house, the tree began to sway more and more. Billy tightened his grip, but the tree kept swaying harder; then it shuddered very hard, and Billy lost his grip.

Billy fell down a few limbs and he grabbed a new hold, but the tree gave another big shake and Billy looked down to the ground and saw Gray Wolf scratching his furry back on the bark of the tree. The harder he scratched, the harder the tree shook. When Billy again lost his hold, down he tumbled, over and over, until finally he landed on a very soft spot. It was even all furry, but it began to move. Billy grabbed two handfuls of fur to secure himself.

Away ran Gray Wolf through the forest with Billy clinging to his back and yelling as loud as he could for Tip. Of course, this frightened the wolf who ran even faster than before, and in just a little while he came out of the trees and there was the lake. "In I go and get rid of this people on my back," thought the wolf. So, he plunged into the water and Billy came up out of the water then: coughing and spitting and sputtering and splashing. He finally stood up and there was Tip, all wet too, and pulling on Billy's jacket and dragging him to shore.

Gran was frantically moving toward her grandson. Running down the path, she screamed to Billy, "Young man, where have you been? I've been looking everywhere. It's too early to swim. Why do you have all your clothes on? Where is the boat?"

Gran picked Billy up in her arms and said, "You must 've fallen in, eh? Well, let's change these clothes and eat those pancakes before they all get cold." Tip was shaking his fur so hard he made water fly everywhere.

"Gran. I have something to tell you," Billy exclaimed. "You'll **never** believe the **fish** I caught this morning!"

Security

Publisher's Note:

Some of the following is written to reflect the dialect of some of the characters—so "spelling errors" you might find are intentional.

Della sat high in the mulberry tree, methodically squeezing the dull bluish-red juice from each berry as she picked it. The juice stained her small sun-tanned hands and ran down in a little purplish river to the dimpled childish elbow. Travler, the half German Shepard and half Collie dog, who had just "arrived" one day, lay on the ground, patiently waiting for his small companion to make her descent.

A lot of thoughts were going through Della's mind today. So many things had happened—changes she didn't understand. She was a child who really thought through things, usually alone. Squeezing mulberries seemed to help the thinking process along, even if her mother did nearly scrub off her hide trying to remove the stains. She thought about the day last week in school when the teacher had made her stand-up in front of the whole fourth grade class, and then had asked her why her arms and hands were that (purple) color.

All the kids laughed, and Della couldn't think of anything to say. She still couldn't. She wondered why Daddy left for work every day now; he didn't use to. Now Uncle Jess had all the work to do around the house, except on Saturdays and Sundays when Daddy stayed home. Daddy was cross all weekend and didn't want Della and Traveler following him around. Uncle Jess didn't mind if they followed him though. Uncle Jess was the one who named Travler. He'd said that's what he was, a "travler." Uncle Jess believed he'd probably travel on some day just like he came, when he was good and ready.

Della hoped not. Travler was her friend. They played together and she could tell him things. She used to be able to tell Mother and Daddy things too, and they would listen. Now they seemed a long way away. Daddy didn't used to be cross. He was happy. Mother used to be pretty too. Now her hair was tied in a knot on top of her head; her mouth wasn't pink and soft anymore. It looked as straight as the vein down the center of the dry leaf Della held in her hand.

Mulberries

Della missed the rides they used to take on Sundays. That's how they had found their ranch. She remembered that day and how they had all felt when they saw the ranch from the highway. If she closed her eyes real tight and tried very hard, she could even remember the feeling she had when Daddy was driving down the lane towards the house. It was almost like magic.

A cloud of fine dust stirred by the car had escorted them along a country lane that was bordered with green alfalfa. It smelled so good; Della had to taste it. It didn't taste nearly as good as it smelled. Daddy said cows liked it, but she couldn't imagine why. Daddy said the alfalfa had to be dried like hay or it would make the cows sick. That was why there was a fence all around it.

The fence didn't stop the little rabbit, though. He had hopped across the lane in front of the car, and if Daddy hadn't stopped so fast, they would have run over the little rabbit. Della wanted to catch it for a pet, but Daddy said it was a wild creature, and Della couldn't run fast enough to catch it. She still thought she could if she'd had the chance.

Della scratched her back on a tree limb and settled back against the old mulberry tree which was doing its best to shield her from the world which she sought to understand. She went back to her reverie anxiously, for this was a happy time to remember.

Daddy had been so excited that first day, and Della could remember the look on his face. It was the same one he used to wear when he brought home surprises in his pockets, or when Mother baked his favorite pie. He had unlatched the gates and driven down the lane like he owned the ranch. Mother asked if he thought the people would mind, and Daddy said he didn't think so.

Mother said a funny thing then. Della had often wondered about it. "Max Miller, your wants show!" Then she said, "Don't you worry. Someday *Miller* will be on a gate." Daddy just laughed, leaned over, and kissed Mother. Then he had looked at Della, smiled, and squeezed her hand.

He said, "Land I want land and land I need. For my Della, I will succeed!" Mother just laughed and shook her head. Della snuggled up to her daddy. Mother understood he loved Della. Whatever he was going to do was all right with her. Mother had a few worry wrinkles when she wasn't laughing at Daddy, but this day they faded away.

Soon the car had come upon another gate. This one was hinged to a fence that encircled the yard and the white house they had seen from the highway. Big trees stood all around the house and Della. had seen the mulberry tree there for the first time. Daddy stopped the car. He got out and stood on the running board and seemed to be looking for something. Then Della saw the old man.

The old man was standing on the front porch of the house and motioning with his arm for them to come the rest of the way. Daddy was so pleased. He unlatched the gate, drove the car through. carefully relatched the gate, and then drove the car up close to the house. He got out and walked over to the man and Della heard him say: "I'm Max Miller; I hope I'm not intruding. We saw your place from the road and just had to have a closer look. It's everything a man could want!"

The old man was bent over like his back hurt, but he was smiling while Daddy was talking. He shook his head and spoke in a funny way. "Nod everyting, my boy, nod everyting. You are nod intruding, no. Mama und me like a little comp'ny no' und den. Gets lonesome, way out here. Bring your family und ve sit on der porch for a while." He turned towards the car and said, "'Vell, come on."

Mother took Della's hand and they walked to the porch where Daddy stood smiling. The old man said: "Himmerling is my name. Come, sit down." He turned towards the screen door and shouted, "Mama, come; .ve have company. Bring some strudel."

Daddy turned to Della and chucked her under the chin with his old rough work-worn hand. "You like strudel, little one?" She wasn't sure what it was, but she nodded her head and smiled a toothless six-year-old grin. The old man laughed. "Aha...ids a goot thing strudel is soft, little one. The goot fairy go'd your teeth. Don't vorry, some new ones vill come for you! .Aha, I vish too some vould come for me also."

Della hoped so too. She liked Mr. Himmerling. He opened the screen door and Mama Himmerling came out of the house with a tray filled with dishes of pink apples oozing out of flaky crusts. She set the tray down on the wide rail around the porch and poured thick yellow cream on each serving of strudel without saying a word.

The sun had disappeared before the Millers went home that day. Mr. Himmerling invited them back for dinner on the next Sunday. Mama Himmerling shook her head in agreement and smiled just a little bit. Della thought she acted like she was dreading something. Even so, Della could hardly wait for the next Sunday. She loved to listen to them talk in their funny way.

Strudel

She went around all week saying *ve* and *goot*, and giggling. Mother laughed with her. Mother also admonished that she must not talk like that around the Himmerlings, because they would think she was making fun of them. She explained they had a German accent because they were likely from Germany.

Mother and Daddy talked all week about the ranch. Daddy wanted to live there; Della knew that. Sunday came. Della got to wear her patent leather slippers and her blue ruffled dress. Mother braided her long hair and put blue ribbons on each braid. When they got to the ranch, Della decided to stay with her mother and watch Mama Himmerling cook. She was fixing a chicken in a big black pot, and she showed Mother how to make dumplings that looked like little clouds floating in the gravy.

Della sat on a stool with her hands folded in her lap and her eyes searched the unfamiliar surroundings as she listened to the two women talk. "You like my kitchen, liebchen? Your face tells me you do. Ah—I as young too I know the want. I still know the want. You have something I wanted. I still want." Her old eyes filled with tears that spilled down her round pink cheeks. She dabbed at them with her apron. "Such an old fool am I. A child—·what would I do with a child—only clutch it close to me and hold it and hold it. You liebchen, you are a child. You will have another someday; you are very young. You are too young to know dat it is everything to have uh child. I tell you—I know."

Della climbed down and walked quietly out the back door. Crying made her sad. She walked carefully, trying not to scratch her shoes. Being a lady was very trying when it lasted and lasted. Della looked all around for Daddy, but she couldn't see him. She went to their car and opened the door. She carefully removed her shoes and peeled off her stockings. She crammed them into the toes of her shoes which she then placed in the center of the car seat. The warm dirt felt good to her bare feet.

She was drawing circles on the ground with her big toe when she was startled by Daddy's call. "Della., come along. Mr. Himmerling is going to take us to the spring. I want you to see it." He looked down at her bare feet end smiled. "Does your mother know about this? Oh well, it's uh warm day. Patent leather isn't too good for walking anyway."

Della trotted along behind her father and Mr. Himmerling. He showed them the pasture which stretched up an incline behind the large barn and sloped towards a place that looked perfect for· a picnic. It was about a mile away. The path they walked was the same one the animals trod. The soil was grooved by many hoof marks.

Della only saw one cow, the old guernsey that Mr. Himmerling called "Bessie." Della walked along the edge of the trail where the dust was thicker. She liked to feel it scatter under her feet, and squish between her toes in tiny little brown puffs. She lagged behind; it was quite a hike for a small girl.

When she came to the spring, Daddy and Mr. Himmerling were sitting on large stones and they were engrossed in conversation. Della flopped down on the grass and rolled over on her back. She picked a yellow topped stalk of sour grass and began to chew on it as she listened. Grownups were always talking.

"You vant to buy my place, ey? Vell, I think ve can arrange something, Max. For a start you come und help me vid de vork. You live here und you learn to be a goot rancher. I'm getting old und da vork I notice more und more. Ve talk later·of buying."

Daddy replied enthusiastically: "Live here, nothing could please me more, but where?·In the barn? It's the only place not filled." Max stood up and looked out over the ranch as Daddy talked: "The chicken houses are overflowing, the fields are green with alfalfa, and the orchards are in bloom." Mr. Himmerling stood up too.

"Oh no! The house is not filled. Ve built it big, for many sons. But they did not come to us. Ve make it into a house for two families."

Della wondered why the sons didn't come. It was too bad because Mr. Himmerling would have made a nice Daddy too. The two men stood together looking at the land. Della was too tired to stand. Daddy shook hands with Mr. Himmerling, then turned around to Della and scooped her up off the grass. "How about a slug of pure spring water to seal that deal, Della my love." He playfully splashed cold clear water on her face, but it felt good. She giggled, and Daddy laughed, and Mr. Himmerling seemed to think it was funny.

Daddy carried Della back down the hill piggy-back style. Part of the way he even galloped. Mama Himmerling didn't seem surprised at the news. She didn't seem pleased either. She said, "Oh Hans, what have you done now?" For a moment Mr. Himmerling was quiet as he looked at his wife. Then he said, "My Frieda, for both of us, I've go'd vat ve vant, don't you see'!" Mama Himmerling said, "Ya, I see, I see, for you Hans, I hope it is right. Come, come, let us eat, and Papa will pray."

Everybody laughed a lot at dinner. Della ate too many dumplings. After dinner, they spent the evening on the front porch making plans to change the house. A kitchen and a bathroom could be added to the back of the old house. The doors between would just be locked; they would soon be neighbors.

Daddy was to come in the evenings and Della and Mother would bring lunch and come along on Saturdays and Sundays to help. Daddy and Mr. Himmerling said it would only take a couple of weeks. The work was to begin right away.

Della couldn't remember for sure how long they worked or just what day it was. It must have been on the weekend sometime, because she and Mother were there. She would never forget how she felt that day. Not even if she lived forever. She covered her face with her hands as she thought about it. She had been trying to climb this same mulberry tree when she had heard the scream. The hammering stopped, and Della ran to the house. She heard Mama Himmerling crying and she could hear her daddy talking in low tones to Hans.

Mother came flying out of the house and ran for the car. She shouted at Della to stay out in back and play until she was called. Della always minded her mother. She decided now was the time to explore the empty barn. She heard her mother start the car and leave in a hurry. She climbed way up in the hayloft end. She found a ladder that led up into a little cupola that extended up above the gambrel-roofed barn. She could see for miles and miles from her perch, the rolling countryside, a ravine farther on, and even old Bessie standing below in the barnyard.

Bessie was standing still, looking far away too. Every now and then her long tail flicked out at flies that tried to rest on her flanks. Della saw her mother's car hurrying back towards the ranch, even before it reached the far end of the lane. She watched it all the way.

A big black car was following her . When they got to the house a man wearing a black hat got out of the big car. He carried a little bag with him and hurried into the house. Later he came out. He looked cross. He shook his head "no." Then he and Daddy shook hands and the man climbed into the big black car and drove away.

"Mr. Himmerling is dead." Daddy said he fell off the ladder and broke his back. Now he was so still in his pretty little bed with the satin pillow. He looked almost the same, but he didn't talk his funny talk anymore. His back wasn't bent anymore either.

Della still couldn't understand exactly where Mr. Himmerling had gone, or what had happened to him. Where do people go when they break their back and they're dead? Della missed Mr. Himmerling.

Mama Himmerling decided to move to the city and live with her sister and nephew. She said the ranch made her too sad. Daddy took her there, and Della was glad when she was gone. Mama Himmerling had just cried and cried and tried to hold Della all the time. She would rock and rock and say over and over again, "Oh Hans, what have you done? It didn't work, it didn't work, I told you so."

Daddy said Mama Himmerling was missing Mr. Himmerling and Della should be very nice to her. Della tried to be nice. She kept thinking when Mama as gone, there would be no more strudel. She thought of strudel and Mama Himmerling at the same time. They were both soft and pink and made you sick if you got too much.

After Mr. Himmerling had passed, they moved to the ranch right away. Daddy was going to run it for Mrs. Himmerling, and maybe buy it when he could. He hired a man to come live there and help him. Daddy said he needed help, because he wasn't much of a rancher yet. Della called the man Uncle Jess.

Uncle Jess wasn't really Della's uncle, but Mother said it sounded better that way. .Anyway, Della liked having an Uncle Jess. Della followed him around when she got home from school. Uncle Jess talked all the time, whether you listened or not. Sometimes Della asked him questions, but it didn't do much good. He didn't seem to listen. So, most of the time she just listened to him.

"No water, that spring's no good. Can't tell your Pa, he thinks this here place is heaven on earth. Poor feller, sure is in for a jolt. 'For long a body won't get a prop'r Saterdy bath round here. One of these here fine days'll see a well driller out here, that's what it'll see."

"Uncle Jess, what's a well driller?"

"Well, it's a driller of wells a course."

Della said, "Oh."

Della rode a bus to school every day. She had to walk the lane though. At first, she was a little afraid, but Daddy said he was too busy to come meet her. Uncle Jess somehow managed to be down in that pasture working every afternoon and just as she got off the bus he always seemed to be finished, so they would go home together.

"Too durn little to walk a mile all by 'er self. Cute young-un, even if she is a pest."

Then one day when Della got off the bus an old dog came to meet her, wagging his tail. Della climbed over the gate and he crawled under it.

"Travler, that's what he is, just like me. We'll bathe that critter if we can find enough water 'round here. Ya won't even know him, he'll be so handsome when we get through."

The dog followed her home, wagging his tail all the way. She looked down at the ground where Travler lay under the tree waiting for her and she was glad he came to her. Daddy had said he could stay if he didn't bother the chickens. Travler was smart. He didn't bother anything. Uncle Jess even taught him to find Bessie and bring her in. Sometimes she got on her high horse, Uncle Jess said, and she'd hide from everybody. Travler always found her though. Daddy thought this was smart for a dog.

One time Bessie hid real good. Everybody looked and looked for her. Daddy was getting real worried. Travler· had to look for a long time, that time. He came running into the yard, though, and he was really barking. Everyone followed him, and they found old Bessie up on the side of the hill hidden in some brush.

Bessie had two little bull calves standing beside her. Della was so excited she nearly exploded. Daddy was mad at Bessie. He wanted a "heifer" or something. Della loved the little twins and she watched them grow every free minute she could spare. The calves drank from old Bessie and they would try to crowd each other out. She would bawl at them, and then they would be good right away.

Uncle Jess said, "She shore could make her young'uns mind good." That was very funny. And Dell thought, "They have to be sold, Della." Daddy said, "Bull calves are good for one thing, money. They'll be before you get home today."

When Della got off the bus, as usual, Travler was waiting for her. She sat down in the dirt and put her arms around his neck and cried and cried. He seemed to understand, he looked sad too.

"Don't cry, child. They didn't suffer none." Uncle Jess was there that day. It was the first time he had worked down there in the afternoon since Travler came. Della felt sad for a long time. She still loved the little twins.

It wasn't long thereafter that they found Bessie in the green alfalfa. Her belly was bigger than it was before the twins came. They called the animal doctor, but he said it was too late. She died. Daddy had said cows liked alfalfa, but it killed Bessie. Della and Travler were sad again.

Mother cried over Bessie too. Della heard her say; "Now what, Max? We have no more money for another cow. Mrs. Himmerling wants her payment. The fruit fell from the trees for lack of water, so there is no money for a payment either. Oh Max, I'm so worried. What are we going to do? Maybe we shouldn't be here."

Daddy had slumped over the table and said, "I don't know, Millie. I don't know. It seems like we've had all bad luck. Cows can be replaced with cows. Springs that go dry must be replaced with wells. I went into town today to see a well driller. He said the aqueduct going through these foothills is ruining a lot of natural springs. We cannot have a well drilled, unless I go back to my old job. If I'm going to save this place, we have to drill a well."

Della opened her eyes and stretched her legs and started picking mulberries. She guessed it wasn't long after Daddy had gone to work, a few weeks maybe, when Mama Himmerling' s nephew came out to see them. He wasn't very nice though. He had a lot of papers in a little suitcase.

Della hurried to the house to hear him talk. He didn't sound like Mr. Himmerling though. She heard him say: "Two weeks, Mrs. Miller. I'm sorry." .Then he got in his big black car and roared away.

"Funny thing: people who drive black cars never smile much," thought Della. Mother just cried. Della tried to put her arms around her, but lately it was hard to do. Mother wasn't feeling very good she guessed. Mother told Della she was going to get a little brother. Della hoped the brother would make Mother happy again.

"Della., Della. Come on down out of that tree. Oh, look at you! Well, that's the last time, anyway. Come on; we'll wash you off in the watering trough. We're about ready to leave, the trailer is already loaded. Get Travler and get in the truck. Uncle Jess handed her his pocket handkerchief to dry herself and walked towards the house without looking back. Della had gotten out of the tree reluctantly. She walked back and touched the trunk and looked up through its spreading branches. Then she turned and ran to the truck. "Come on Travler! Let's go."

The old truck bumped slowly down the lane. The trailer full of their belongings jolted in its path. Mother wiped her eyes and blew her nose. Daddy stopped for the last gate and Uncle Jess got out to open it, and he dragged his suitcase along with him. He pulled Della's pigtail and said, "You be good., you hear! Oh, here's a collar I made for that old hound a' yours."

Uncle Jess allowed the truck to pass through, then carefully latched the gate barring the lane behind them. He walked to the side of the truck and shook hands with Daddy. "I'm gonna look over to this other place and see if they have any work. You all take care now." He tipped his hat to Mother and blew a kiss to Della who returned it with a great flourish of hand waving and teary goodbyes.

Daddy leaned over and kissed away Mother's tears. He said, "Liebchen, don't cry anymore. He gently laid his hand on her swollen stomach and smiled. We're leaving with more than we came with, I can tell you dat!"

The old truck chugged around the bend. The ranch was out of sight. Della suddenly sat up very straight and her tears stopped. "Daddy, you're right. We have Travler now. Uncle Jess said he'd leave, but Travler's smart!"

Travler raised his head at the sound of his name and thumped his tail on the floor of the truck.

Sixteen

The sore throat was better, so after a lot of pleading, I could go to the Roller Rink on Friday night. This was the big night of the week, all the kids met at the Roller Rink and sometimes the most exciting people were there.

On this particular Friday a busload of young Airmen from March Air Base was there. One of the most exciting nights of my life transpired.

He was all of nineteen and looked so handsome in his uniform. He was blond, shy and good-looking and not a very accomplished skater. He had a Southern drawl that made my heart beat faster, so we sat together and spent most of the evening in conversation. He was from Georgia and had never been away from home until he joined the Air Force. I was a senior in High School and it hadn't been so long since he had been one. We found we had a lot in common and we laughed a lot together.

My girlfriend kept coming by and trying to pry me loose, with little success. It wasn't long though until 10:00 P.M. rolled around and Jimmy had to go. I had really started to get my sore threat and headache again, so we all decided it was time to go, but Jimmy asked me for a date the following Friday. That was to be a "real" date. So, I gave him my address and went home smiling.

By Monday morning my relapse was serious. I hurt all over; my temperature was steady at 102 and I was really ailing. I saw the doctor who instigated a whole series of tests I didn't feel like participating in.

Heavy antibiotics were prescribed which made me sick to my stomach in addition to everything else. My legs ached so badly I cried if anyone bumped my bed. My illness was diagnosed as Rheumatic Fever and my life changed.

Not knowing how to reach Jimmy, I had to wait in despair for his arrival home on the following Friday. I arranged my hair on top of my head the best I could, not having been allowed a shampoo. I applied my makeup rather shakily and dressed in my most glamorous cotton PJs. I fluffed my pillows and waited.

Finally, Jimmy arrived and seemed somewhat surprised; however, he was just as nice as he had seemed before. Even my father was impressed. We were allowed a thirty-minute visit, but we made a date for another Friday night two-weeks away. He left and said he'd be back. I could hardly wait.

On the next Friday evening there was another young airman at our door. He spoke to my father and left a letter for me. It was from Jimmy, according to his friend. Jimmy's unit had been shipped out and he was not allowed to contact anyone. He had asked his friend to deliver his brief note which simply said he was unable to keep our appointment and he would explain later. He never did. In fact, I never heard from him or about him again.

The war was over in about a year. My illness was never completely over. One of the aftermaths was a little ol' heart murmur. Almost fitting somehow. I sure hope Jimmy got home to Georgia.

Where's Charlie?

Simon lowered his aching arthritic old bones onto the park bench. He had carefully chosen the bench that afforded the best point of observation. Here in the Plaza, a man could warm himself in the sun and listen to the bubbling fountain while he watched the parade pass by. Besides, most of his friends came here during the day. Charlie would be here in a little while.

Simon patted the small box of miniature checkers in his pocket. He wiped off the coffee'd mustache that hid his toothless gums. He stretched luxuriously, still tasting the hot creamed brew and dunked toast he'd had for breakfast. He looked up at the sky and paid homage to the sun.

Simon reached into his frayed suit coat pocket and brought out the toast crusts he's saved for the pigeons. They were all gathered around him on the bench and at his feet, impatiently waiting for the daily ritual feeding.

The boldest of the lot was precariously perched on Simon's shoulder. He inclined his head and with his red eyes stared at Simon, waiting to see where it would be his pleasure to hide the largest cracker today.

Simon laid the piece of toast on the brim of his hat and the pigeon snatched it up and flew away among the chattering and screeching of his contemporaries who risked less and got the same.

Simon laughed aloud and was surprised at the sound. He painstakingly doled out the rest of the booty until the crumbs of bread were all gone. The pigeons did not hesitate; they knew the minute the party was over, and they lingered not. The fluttering of wings signaled their departure to meet another benefactor.

"I wonder where ole Charlie is?" thought Simon. He looked at the clock that stood in front of the jewelry store across the street. "Ole Charlie's most always here by now."

A young sailor had been standing on the corner for a long time. There were so many that hung around the Plaza that Simon didn't usually spend time watching them. This one seemed anxious about something. Simon eyed him casually. The sailor shaded his eyes against the morning sun and peered down the street. He had eyes only for whatever it was he as searching for. He ignored the flashy marquee on the theatre across from the jewelry store. "Sex World" and "Love for the Asking" as the double-bill advertised in large letters. Two eight-foot buxom paper dolls stood in front of the theatre; they looked as if they were waiting patiently for someone to cover their black lace undies with clip-on dresses.

Simon scrutinized the beauties and rubbed his hands together. Once again, he stretched his body out in the sun. His movement reminded him of all his birthdays and the futility of his longing. He laid his hand on his groin and went back to watching the sailor.

"Must be kinda hard for sailor boys, no pockets to put their hands into," thought Simon. "I wonder what he's waiting for, standing at that bus stop. He never gets on. That's three buses he's let go by. Another one is pulling in now."

The bus wheezed to a stop and the sailor looked expectantly at the exit door. A young woman carrying a new black pasteboard suitcase stepped off. She looked around and saw the sailor. Simon watched the girl sedately set down her suitcase behind the waiting bench. Then she walked towards the sailor with her hands held in front of her, palms stretched upward. The sailor just stood there waiting. The sun sparkled on the tears that made their way down his shiny, youthful face. He reached for the girl and tenderly folded her in his arms He buried his face in her neck and the two figures appeared as one. Humanity smiled as it passed on either side.

The girl finally stepped back and took the sailors hands in hers. Simon heard her say, "People are staring at us." She looked around and saw Simon smiling.

"And that old man is leering at me."

Simon tried to look away, but he couldn't afford to lose these tender moments; he blinked his old eyes and watched anyway. He heard the sailor say, "So am I! God, Dolly, you don't know how I've dreamed of this day. I just can't believe you're here. Come on, Honey. I've got us a. room."

He picked up her bag and they hurriedly walked away; their hands gripped tightly together.

It took a few minutes for Simon to find his way back to reality. The dreamy world he was in offered a great deal of promise. He laid both hands over his groin in a protective manner and dropped his chin on his chest, closing out the world.

He thought of Mary. It was so long ago. He could still remember the softness of her skin and her warm and gentle yielding. Mary always smelled like sunshine. He longed for their feather bed and the way she let him curl around her and cup her small pointed breasts in his hands.

"Hey Simon, what the devil are you doing? Hee hee hee..."

Simon snapped out of his reverie and looked up at Toby. Tobacco juice ran from the edges of Toby's mouth, and he wore a crumpled, dirty old hat pushed back on his bald head.

"I sneaked up on you that time."

"Well, you approached me from down wind or you wouldn' a surprised me," said Simon.

"Hee hee hee," cackled Toby. "Where's Charlie today? Want somebody to play checkers with ya, huh? I'll play ya a game, Simon."

Simon wondered where his friend was. He glanced again at the clock. It was 12:30 already. He dug in his pocket and fished out fifty cents. He handed it to Toby and said, "Go across the way there, and get us a bottle of Tokay. Bring it back too, you hear?"

Toby took the money quickly and answered, "Sure, Simon. You know I will ol' buddy pal." Simon tried to slip back to his dream, but voices pulled him out again.

"By God, Nell, I told you no and no it is." A man's voice spoke evenly and firmly. The woman he spoke to walked slowly by his side. She was as tall as her man and she wore a tight black dress which strained to retain her female charms. Her red hair was fluffed out around her painted face and she clung to her man's arm as though she were drowning.

"Please Daddikins, I'm good to you, now aint I? Just think what that dress 'd do for your Nell!" A small girl child was following in their wake. She smiled at Simon. He gestured with his hand for her to come over to him. She walked slowly towards him. Her gray eyes never blinking nor her smile slipping. She stood in front of him waiting patiently. "Hullo Baby, what's your name?"

The child continued to smile as she stared at Simon, but no sound did she make.

"Whatcha got in your hand?" Both her fists were tightly clamped, and Simon gestured towards the one she held behind her. She opened the one she held in front of her for him to see, her eyes never blinking or leaving his face. "Oh, bread huh? Want to feed the pigeons?"

Simon reached for the bread and was surprised when he touched the child's hand. "You're cold, Baby. Aint you got no sweater? This sun ought to do a young'un though."

Simon looked up at the sky to be sure the sun he referred to was still shining. The child allowed him to take the bread from her open hand. The pigeons flocked to the feast. The brazen one landed again on Simon's shoulder and took the lion's share. "There, how do you like that?" said Simon. The birds fluttered away when his hands were emptied.

"They always leave when I run out of food. Can you talk?"

There was no answer. The smile persisted on the baby face. Simon looked into the somber gray eyes and saw his own reflection. He took the little girl's hand in his own and said,

"Come closer over here, Baby. You're so cold." The child shuddered, but obediently moved closer to the old man's side.

"Get away from that dirty old man! God, I'll have to scrub the hide off you. I spose he's had his clammy old hands all the hell over you! Mike, call the cops. This old beggar's been gettin' fresh with the kid. I know what you're up to fella. I met a few old beggars in my own time, see."

Nell grabbed the child by the arm and jerked her away from Simon. People stopped on the sidewalk and stared and then hurried on. The man called Mike tried to quiet his woman.

Simon implored, "She's so cold, Mister. I was only tryin; to get her warm. I wouldn't hurt the Baby, Mister." The man said nothing to Simon. He just gathered up his women and hurried them away.

"Never mind Nell, she's O.K. What's the difference anyhow. She don't know one end from the other."

"You ought a know," screamed Nell. Now that the new dress was under her arm, her voice was no longer placating. The two walked down the street arguing, the child still in their wake.

"Here's the hotel, ole buddy pal. I told you Toby'd bring it back. Charlie not here yet?" Toby handed the sack to Simon and smacked his lips in expectation. Simon opened the bottle carefully being sure it remained hidden in the sack. He took a long swig.

He closed his eyes and let the wine run down his throat and warm his chilled insides. He handed the bottle to Toby and reached in his pocket for his checkers. He spread the little checkered oil cloth on the bench and carefully placed the checkers in order. Red for him, black for Toby.

Simon looked around again for Charlie. he mused to himself, "I wonder where ole Charlie is. -I'd be drinking with him."

"Ah, Simon ol' buddy pal, I like the red best," pleaded Toby. Simon silenced his companion with a glance and moved a checker out into the field of battle at the same time. Toby handed back the bottle and Simon wiped off the mouth with his coat sleeve before he took another long drink. This emptied the bottle and Simon handed it to Toby to throw away before they were caught with it in the Plaza.

It galled Simon for Toby to get a man to the king row before he could. His reputation as "Checker Champ of the Plaza" was in danger, and of all the bums, Toby was the worst to lose to.

Simon couldn't think clearly about the game. He kept seeing the little girl's gray eyes above her perpetually smiling face. Simon lost three checkers in a triple jump and Toby cackled and clapped his big hands. Simon tried very hard to be nonchalant.

Then Simon loudly queried so everyone could hear and understand: "Any of your boys seen Charlie today? I could be playing with the guy if Charlie would get hisself down here where he belongs."

The Plaza group which had gathered around to watch the game all shook their heads no. The afternoon air was getting chilly. The fog was being sucked across the warm land and Simon could feel the dampness of the sea settle around him.

"Hee hee hee... I beat cha! Two out 'a three? That's what I done; I beat cha." Old Toby pulled his hat down to a jaunty angle and said, "Let's play another game, Simon. I'll go easy on ya this time."

Simon shook his shaggy head no and gathered up his checkers. He carefully placed them in their box and then he slowly rose off the bench. He shoved the checker box in his pocket and started to walk away.

"Y'er mad cause I beat cha," snarled Toby.

"No," said Simon. "I gotta go find that damn Charlie."

The Author

Joy Sorrell in 2020 at The Manor in San Diego
(Portrait by Robyn Scherer Photography,
www.robynschererphotography.com)

All of these stories (including Aunt Lola sitting in the pumpkin pie)
were written a long time ago. How time flies!
These treasures I dedicate to my two sons, the "joy" of my life.

--*Joy Sorrell*

About Manor Publishing Collective

Sunny Baker (center) with Manor Residents
in San Diego, CA in 2019

MPC: A NEW KIND OF PUBLISHER:

EXCLUSIVELY FOR SENIORS OVER 60

The Manor Publishing Collective (MPC), founded by Sunny J. Baker, Ph.D., is a notable non-profit venture of former and would-be authors who want to share their ideas, experiences, and creativity with the world—but who don't want (or need) to master the technologies of the 21st Century to make it happen.

Sunny has background in computers and success writing 28 traditional books, some of them bestsellers, with conventional publishers. Because of her experience, she's able to produce the books, design the covers, and complete the marketing (with occasional help from publishing and marketing interns). The other members of the collective, all over 60, and currently with an average age over 80, simply write and create!

The shared royalties (a portion of each author's earnings in a collective account) earned by the authors are exactly that—shared by all members of the collective.

Please support these amazing creatives and their community by looking for and reading (and purchasing) all the publications by MPC authors at http://amazon.com/author/manorcollective.

DO YOU HAVE SOMETHING YOU'D LIKE PUBLISHED?

If you are a senior with your own books, stories, poems, photographic compilations, or memoirs in drawers, files or shoeboxes, you can learn more about becoming an MPC author at booksbyseniors.org.

We would love to hear from you.

—Sunny Baker, Publisher and Founder

Manor Publishing Collective